DATE DUE

DEMCO 38-297

GRANITE LADY

Granite Lady

POEMS

Susan Fromberg Schaeffer

Macmillan Publishing Co., Inc.

NEW YORK

Macmillan Publishing Co., Inc.
866 Third Avenue, New York, N. Y. 10022
Collier-Macmillan Canada Ltd.

Library of Congress Cataloging in Publication Data
Schaeffer, Susan Fromberg.
      Granite lady.

      I. Title.
PS3569.C35G7 1974b   811'.5'4   73-21294
      ISBN 0-02-607010-3

FIRST PRINTING 1974

PRINTED IN THE UNITED STATES OF AMERICA

For Linda Lerner, Tuuli-Ann Ristkok,
and the memory
of S. Ronald Weiner

With special thanks to Jules Gelernt, for his time and insight.

ACKNOWLEDGMENTS

Some of the poems in this volume first appeared in the following maga-
zines, to whose editors grateful acknowledgment is made: *The American
Scholar, Arion's Dolphin, Boundary 2, Carleton Miscellany, Chelsea, En-
counter, Epoch, Far Point, Florida Quarterly, The Humanist, Jeopardy, Jesture
Magazine, Little Magazine, Lotus, Mediterranean Review, New Statesman,
The Ohio Review, Resonance, The Sceptre Press, South Dakota Review,
Three Rivers Journal*. "Suicide" was first published in *Poetry*. "Age" was
first published in *Esquire Magazine*. "To Someone Who Was Never Un-
happy or Afraid," "Valentine to the Sun," and "Reading the Signs" were
first published in *College English* and are reprinted by permission of the
National Council of Teachers of English. "Transitions" was published in
College English, March 1974, and is reprinted by permission of the National
Council of Teachers of English.

Contents

IV. Lightning Storm

V. Immortalities

VI. Sleeplust

VII. *The Bridge*

VIII. *Reading the Signs*

I. Winter

WINTER

In the winter season
The trees stand up like nerves.

Whatever they have done
They tell the sky.
The sky soaks up their tears.

In the winter season
People go in behind dead wood.
Their nerves coat their bodies

Like very fine net.
This does not show in mirrors,
The tattoo that seems to surface
Developing itself

On the print of the skin,
The map.

In the winter season
They have nothing but clothes
And each other

And spring arrives for them
With razors and knives.

AFTERWARDS

After the misery
And the remembrance of misery

After the pain
And the memory of pain

After the salt pool that points
Or seems to point
Toward the sea

After the white tinge of salt
        on shoes
After the salt of bones
        into the earth

What is there to say?
The sublime?

        I have looked on God's legions, and lived?
        I have looked on it all, and gone blind?

The ridiculous?

        I have cooked food for the soul from a mix?
        I have starved the soul like a dog?
        It obeys.

The design in the carpet comes clear.
Now you see it, would you decide
Your life, that one thread,

Should pull free?

II. Glimmerings

THE DOOR

When my head touches the pillow, the voices start.
They are outside the door, so I can't tell how many there are.
They keep saying how much they will do; they will help me get out.
One says she will dissolve herself
And come under the door like a gas,
Another will melt herself down like a wax,
Take a cast of the key to slide under the door,
Or throw herself like a stone through a sharp pane of glass,
Though this may mean slashing her wrists.

I wake up and tell them in whisper or hiss
I like the room just as it is, with its four walls
Like four book jackets, holding their stories in.
Before, the mirrors were up, leaning in, smudged
By the fingers and thumbs, noses and lips,
Holes in strong wood, thick as prints on a drinking glass
Too many people had kissed, and when the wind came up,
The curtain would grope through the room
Like a dangerous hand.
Now the mirrors are gone, and the window is shut.

The voices are at it again, having their say.
I tell them, I was told to stay here, and I will.
I remind them how all the rivers drip into the seas
And flow through the mouths of the sharks,
How the topmost boughs always crack under my weight,
How someone has always sawed through one of the rungs,
And how the beaks of the buzzards wait in the peaks
Of the day for the sped vessels lighter than air.

Then they shut up. But soon they come back with their props,
The circus balloon, the white rabbit pulled like a cloud
From the sky's flat blue hat, the shroud to go over
The magician's girl who then will grow whole
(She won't get up, but sleeps like a dress in a trunk)
And Christ dancing in the suit of the lumbering bear.
Now they are singing of the world and its pearls;
They are offering me one, like a sweet or a drug.
I am in the cradle, and I am going to stay.

They are gnashing their teeth;
They are telling me terrible tales
Of the cardboard beasts circling my bed, and the sun,
Hung in the sky like a toy, more than just warm.
They are warning me of the walls, and how they move in.
They are crowded and cramped; their paper dresses are torn.
They lust for the halls of the carpeted skull.
They are starved to be born.

GLIMMERINGS

In the beginning was the mother.
There were planets in her eyes.
In her mouth, there were glistening cliffs.

Behind the cliffs was a shiny red animal
Who popped out when she wanted it
And went right back in. It was her pet,
And entirely tame.

She could make the room
Blink night and day, just like eyes.
She was a great tree,
Holding the world in her branches

And everything on her was growing.
She had two pink tongues on her chest.
The child's own head was cornsilk
But the mother's was covered with vines.

She waved her hands over it;
It turned into a tail. She bent over,
There was a nice smell, the light went right out.
She stood in the door in front of a light,
She was entirely black, charred like a tree.

She stood in the door with the light falling
On her; she caught it in her hands.
She glowed like a bulb, electric,
She was an angel, she was hiding her wings.

Her arms and legs were covered with strange roots
That wiggled. The child knew they could grow
Deep down into the floor, and the mother
Could grow up and up, her hair

Spreading out and out, darkening into night.
Perhaps she did this every night
While the child was asleep. The child felt fortunate

The mother seemed to take an interest
In her little plot, where she was planted
Like a bush.
How she was watered!
How she was fed!
She prospered; she learned to walk.

She had no idea!
The mother had a room full of shiny white boxes.
Inside of one lived four small blue animals
With hot coats of fur you never could touch.

The mother could make them come and go
By twisting a button.
She could make them grow up, or down.
The child felt they were afraid of the mother.
Most of the time they hid.

The mother had boxes of sticks with red and blue heads.
She waved her hands over, and tiny blue babies
Made their appearance. They were just like the ones
On the shining white box, but they died right away,
"Burning down," said the mother,

Curling up like the new infant, still in his crib.
The mother threw them out, black little bodies,
Leaving their ashy flesh on her hands.
The child thought maybe they grew somewhere else later.
She hoped the four animals in the box did not take it badly.

The mother had another box, empty,
Made of something just like her teeth.
The mother could make water come out of its neck
Whenever she wanted, and when she was through,

She just twisted it hard.
The child began to feel fear.
The mother could call up a lake
And put her right in it.

It was slippery, like teeth, and she felt like a tongue.
Perhaps she would be left here forever.
The mother came and got her.

[10]

They went out for walks.
The mother would look slyly at the buildings
With the eye of a crow.

Finally, she came to the one that she wanted.
She gave something to the man sitting in a glass box.
He smiled back quite strangely.
Inside, it was dark.

People were sitting inside like pegs in a block.
The child knew better than to start crying now.
On the wall, there were fires, and rainstorms,
And animals that talked. In the air,

Was a pathway of light looking quite like a road
Though nothing walked on it.
The fires ran after the animals, and the animals
Ran away. Sometimes, the wall showed a witch
Cooking an apple. Sometimes,

It showed a girl lying in a glass case
And little men who watched it.
Then she came out of the box.

The mother looked well pleased.
When they went out, the mother knew how
To make men give her things from the glass cases.
The child was impressed, and also afraid.

When they got home, the mother turned on the water
And called up the four beasts called *fire*.
The child saw the mother could flood the whole place;
She saw herself sailing down the stairs
And into the street in her little yellow boat.
She often was bad.

She saw her mother's teeth start grinding an apple.
She waited all day, feeling afraid.
Nothing happened.

She bit into an apple,
And one of her teeth stuck right in it.
She broke another on a piece of water
Her mother had turned into ice.

The child began to feel fear of the mother
Watching her move about the house like a powerful wall,
Her hands full of switches.
She was beginning to be afraid.
She was beginning to be seen, and not heard.
She hoped the mother was nice.

TEETHING

The child does not visit its mother.
An ordinary enough situation.

The mother complains of her lot.
This is understood.

As the years pass,
The child brings home her old clothes

Which get smaller and smaller.
These the mother dismembers

For zippers and buttons.
She knows she is plundering the grave

Of the living.
At night, the child opens her purse,

Sees her quarters
Have turned into milk teeth

Roots stained, blood
Rusty-red.

The mother flies out through
The wall ribs, neon blue skeleton,

Her dress stitched down with quarters.
In the full moon, they gleam, cold sequins.

In the morning, the child wakes up poor.

ALPHABET

The child sat on one side of the table in the kitchen,
The mother on the other,
Her whole face round and blank, like a zero,
Her two eyes blank slots of a pinball machine.

The child's arm was her handle, thin as a chicken's.
Whenever she moved it, the long row of images
Began moving and rolling, first slowly, then racing,
In the slot machine eyes.

The mother's housedress looked innocent,
Covered with kittens, eyes boggled above whiskers,
Worn by the iron, frayed by the bleach,
Tied tight at the waist,

But at the wrong answers, they could turn
Lions and tigers, giving their growls.
This was a gamble; the child knew it well.
This was the lesson called homework.

The child wanted to draw an a.
It was fat, like a kitten, rump in the air,
Paws tucked under, trailing its tail.
It was sweet, like the tadpoles that turned into frogs;

It was friendly, like a mouse standing up for a talk,
A nice little apple, threaded with stem.
She would draw it in all 48 colors from her *Crayola* box.
The white paper was as ready to receive it
As a sheet in a crib.

She was as hopeful as a birthday.
She told her mother what she wanted.
The mother picked up a pencil; she had pared it
Like an apple with the sharpest of knives.

Without hesitation, she drew it: A.
The child shook her head.
This was not what she wanted.
There it stood, legs spread apart,

Arms across its chest, breastless, no curves at all,
Wearing the pointed hat of a dunce, or a witch,
Or a soldier.
It was all disapproving, a teepee, barred at the door.

Its feet dug into the earth
Like two spikes of pencils. It wasn't going anywhere.
It would be insulted in white.
It would look silly in yellow.

The child shook her head. She tried hard explaining.
The mother lurched across the table,
Grabbing her hand. She grabbed it so hard
She broke the crayon in two, *cerulean blue.*

Hand on hand, she forced the child to draw an A
With the stub.
The child screamed; she tore up the paper.
The mother pinned her down; she gave her another sheet

Blanker than the window square watching.
She gave her the crayon called *aquamarine.*
The child was still and ugly as a toad.
The mother conjured up meals disappearing.

They were sliding back into the oven, the vacuum of time,
The child's own bones stacked in a box like the crayons.
The child tried to draw it again, her favorite letter.
She couldn't quite get it, its head open and gashed.

She started to cry. The mother slapped her, leaving two marks.
They had taken the locks from the bathroom and bedroom.
There was nowhere to hide.
The mother picked up a hanger, and began beating her, hard.

The child cried for hours.
She saw the pots, hanging on the nails like helmets,
Handles handy for twisting off enemies' heads.
She saw the long shiny knives, and the long fork

With two fangs. She saw the supper, like Snow White,
Behind the glass case. She gave up.
She took her black crayon and drew it: A.
The mother's eyes started whirling and clacking,

Reels of fruit flashing, also skulls and white crossbones,
And solid gold stars. She opened her mouth,
Coins poured out in rivers, all silver, and out of her ears.
When they hit the floor, they melted like ice.

When the child looked at her hand
She could see every blue vein in it.
They all wove into letters, as if embroidered in thread.
She kept seeing her mother covered with knives,
Her Christmas orange, punctured with cloves.

Of course, said the mother,
Picking up a napkin and a piece of a crayon,
There is also this kind: and she drew it: a.
The child lowered her head onto the table,

Right onto her plate, a spoon by one ear,
A knife and fork by the other.
The vertebrae on her neck showed through quite clearly.
If you knew how to count, you could count them.

This was the first lesson.
There would be 26 more.

THE MOTHER'S CURSES

The Mother's house was always well stocked with curses.
She stored them in the cabinet, neatly stacked

In jars of spinach and corn; they lay just under
The protective layer of wax over the strawberry jam,

But the most powerful and the best
Were kept in rows of ice cubes, neat in their trays.

These her child was forbidden to touch,
But she had seen them, and frozen in each one

Was a tiny child, looking just like herself.
The Mother was keeping these for emergencies;

She was biding her time. Whenever the child was bad,
The Mother would go to the box, and say,

"May you have a child just like you,"
And threaten to pull out the plug, and the child

Would be beside herself with fear. Finally,
The child grew up and had a Child,

And the mother was happy. Then the child grew afraid
And went to the icebox of the Mother.

Sure enough, one of the cubes was gone;
The mother stood by, licking her lips.

The child began to examine her child as if she were something
That lived on a slide. She tried coaxing the sun

Into her monocle, and into her magnifying glass;
There was no doubt about it: the resemblance was strong.

Everyone commented on it; the mother grew taller and plumper,
And grinned ear to ear. The child tried to teach her Child

To make faces, to wear lipstick, to pluck her eyebrows,
Anything at all. Nothing came of it. Everyone said,

"She looks just like her mother." Finally, the child
Grew used to living with the sword and the moon hanging

Just over her head. She decided, "So what if it falls?
I've lived a long time, and worried more than a God."

She had another Child, this time a boy,
And everyone said he looked just like his father,

And though another cube was missing from the ice tray
The Mother began wrinkling, and stooping, and complaining

Of arthritis, and how she could hardly lift an arm over her head.
The child was relieved, and began to take pleasure

When people said her Child looked just like her mother,
But one day, she came home early with bags full of groceries,

And found her Child staring into the cubes,
Her face frozen in horror, and the child went to look,

And in each cube, there She was, and her Daughter
Backed away from her, was stuck to the wall like wallpaper,

Was glued there with fear.
Then the child put her head on her arms and cried

And agreed with her Daughter to cover the mirrors;
She didn't know how: it had happened again.

SKULL SONG

I am sitting here in the sun
Watching the kittens playing
And the children playing
And I am convinced
There is nothing worth doing more.
The sun,
Which has a bad habit of burning everything up,
Is burning up the past
Like a thick, shrouding fog.

If the children ask me why
I am putting flowers in the skull
Of my mother,
I say, *it looks better that way*,
I say, *why not?*
And now when they draw on it with their crayons
As they will draw on mine later
I do not scold them.

III. Apples

MAY LEVINE

Grandmother, the same hot night you died
Our house burned down.
Sweet cynic ghost, it did.
Before that, we sat round
Our Aunt's old table.
You were the sugar stirring in our tea,
The pattern on our plates.

That night, my mother had a dream.
In the Bedford-Stuyvesant brownstone house,
She stood in the white closet.
Red saucers were stacked on red plates.
One was cracked. She frowned.
Her grandmother, braids coiled
And fastened with a diamond clip,
Said not to worry that May was late;
Coffee and cake would keep.
Uncle Bill said the same; Manny too.
My mother woke and smiled.
The next morning she frowned to see
What her dream meant.
All, all were dead.
The shades, the beloved shades
Were welcoming the newly dead.

May Levine,
I did not dream, but coming home
I saw the steps to my attic room
Burned and blackened. The rail was gone.
Grandmother, while we were children
We never knew that fire burned,
Much less consumed.
Your petalled hands soothed our wounds,
Such dolls, such songs,
We burned, but not for long.
Grandmother, Grandmother, childish, at last
You became a doll to us.
They have put you back in your box.
Now you fall from me
Like childhood's petals,
Hot crimson tulips,
You leave your warmth.
We never knew you scorched till you burned up.

Now I am the one who wakes to watch
In the watchful night.
Asbestos of my youth, cold ghost,
I would see you rest.
In the next room my mother stirs.
House of my childhood, drawbridge to this,
Again through dark corridors
You go first.

TO MY GRANDMOTHER, IN A HOME

Through the convex glass of our regret,
We saw each sign of frost and freezing,
Her frozen smile, like ice, cracking as we left,
But were slower to see the signs of spring and thaw:
That before her smile ignited for us, first
The smile she had for others had to fade and die.
We noticed instead how her mind lost ground,
Charting her senility as navigators do maps,
We wanted to know where she strayed, and how far.

She fled from us through an undiscovered ocean,
And big fish with carnal teeth and jaws
Swallowed her little fish thoughts. At the door,
We saw her, bewildered fish, nose to the aquarium's wall,
Like some pale paper lantern drifting without a string,
Or some deep sea creature bleached by time,
The depth, and our neglect, sinking slowly through
The layered sea, beneath our antique childhoods,
Then beneath her own, while we imagined her,
Old scavenger, searching the splinters
Of a shipwrecked life. And so we did not notice
When first she turned from us smiling,
But one day, looking back, we saw in the shining door
The brilliant ripples of a cloudless sky.

Ancient fish of cartilege and bone, who, when young,
Loved only in her own image, her children and grandchildren,
She sank through a layered ocean where fish ate her labels
And her categories, and heard what she had never heard
The siren song of salt-blood to salt-blood,
Turning the pebbles of her mind to opalescent pearls
Or sequined rainbow fish. She joined a school
Of delicate glass-fragile creatures, and learned
To swim in complex, sharing patterns,
Until one day, looking toward the surface of the sea,
She saw the sun
A crimson flower floating its petals on the waters,
And at night, the moon a silver dandelion gone to seed.
And so again we follow her, our grandmother,
Through deepening, deepening waters,
Dear pilot fish, who must be eaten by the shark.

A GRANDMOTHER ALONE

For three weeks, since my grandfather's death,
She has lived alone
Bricked and Brooklyned in behind the bricks and stones
Of that old house where she has always lived.
The curtains are drawn
And inside it is all
Maroon and velvet dark.
The furniture was not to fade, nor has it done
And every table with its mirror top
Still reflects the crystal waterfall of each rainbow lamp
And their pink-ribboned fluted cupcake shades.
Crystal swans arch their necks on mirror lakes,
Smug on their reflections, upside-down,
And a beam of golden dust
Is pollen on the carpet's purple bloom,
Perpetual and lush. Gilt cherubs beat their innocent wings,
And on the walls are strung
Watercolors of gardens formal as Versailles,
Pines like ice-cream cones,
Their avenues, whittled by perspective's blade,
Diminished to triangles or sharp knives.

Something cuts her off.

The ribs of the house flex and crack,
And every sound a new round through the house.
No light seems bright enough. At night,
Under a grinning moon and skimming clouds,
She feels white walls thin and thin.
Invisible armies march up the stairs
To grimace at her bed.
Clothes stir in the closets, blackly, like ghosts,
And corners darken past the blackness of mere night.
Her old hand cradles the phone, her black friend,
Old umbilicus to four children, long grown, long gone.
On the porch, the green swing squeaks and creaks
Bearing a weight she dare not guess,
And above it, the striped awning inhales the storm, flaps
And collapses, a worn-out lung.

During the day, she rocks in her old chair,
Her head pressed against the gilt cornucopia
Stencilled on its rim.
The mirrors fill with birthdays, holidays,
The family gathered around the oval table,
An ark against a lifetime's floods.
Under the waxed mahogany, candles float and flicker.
Water spills to the floor, laughter tinkles in the chandelier,
Cakes disappear, the carrots, ignored, grow cold,
Beading butter in drops of golden wax.
But it ends, it ends,
There is nothing to clean up,
No boots to put on
The children on the stairs, in tiers,
Like figures on a wedding cake, the two smallest at the top
Melted, like wax, together.
No wet kisses, quarrels, last goodbyes
And the old question: You'll come back when?

She remembers now
A mirror in her daughter's burnt-out house
Veil after smoky veil
And all she could see was her own face
Moon-white, a lantern floating on a smoky sea.
No mirror could reflect all her life.
Now things reverse themselves.
Gilded picture frames, the mirrors
Hold the old images, the old scenes.
Ghostly moving men climb her stone stairs
Empty her house chair by chair.
The rooms of her mind empty, quickly, like old cooky jars.
Evicted, victim of her white hair, she moves
Through the looking glass from an unfurnished present
To a furnished past.
Despair is dispossession, emptiness.
Alone in a corner, beneath a bare window frame
The arcs of her rocker creak
Against the dry planks of the floor.
She sets her table with one plate,
Eats slowly, slowly, as if
Every supper were her last.

NEWBORN

Out of the cradle
Goes the baby,
The small one, the fish,
The cross-eyed,

Into it, yourself.
Each day, sea creature,
Scale creature,
One barnacle slips from your skin.

Now it is clear you are gold.
And the memories!
He is the magic word,

The Open Sesame, the Shazam.
Your great-grandmother
Sits on the sand,
Spreads
Her voluminous skirt

Blankets, dark wings.
Sobriety and darkness.
She sets down your mother.

They watch the water.
It winks.
Glare of the water.
She moves the child from her right.

The sky
Gleams with its blues,
The water, deep quilt of greens.
Suddenly,

The boardwalk lets sail
A black car.
It is elegant and gleams.
It flies through the air,

Canonized penguin,
Car and driver
Fish mouths slit wide.

Thin wheels, tracks in the sand,
The running board grazing
Your great-grandmother's side,
The child pressing her other.

No one is harmed.
Your mother

Stares at the car and its man,
The funny new gods.
World of possibilities and miracles.
Your grandfather's ivories

Rising out of the sea.
The past which glittered
And was gold.
The past, the real sin,

How we cast it in iron,
God-objects of gold.
I can see

The Model T's, the Overlands,
The Stutz Bearcats
Driving the ocean,

Steering the conches, the squid,
The driver, his goggles,
The cap with its visor,

The sweet rumble seat.
It is Sunday
And the water is fine.

Benjamin, your hair shines gold
As the key you just gave me.
You take my grandfather's hand.

I'm holding to Grandma.
Here is the land
They died just in sight of.

They are coming clear,
Two fish rising up.
They speak all in bubbles.

We are walking together
Out of this last world of sand.

APPLES

God only knows
(If he knows anything at all
About our lives and deaths),

Why we bought these seven
Styrofoam apples,
Red-flocked.

Now they hang over you,
Seven red planets,
A constellation of sorts.

They revolve in the winds,
The currents of the blood
Eat them.

They are no angry planets.
They are pomegranates,

Red hearts of blood.
While you watch them,
They beat.

Embryo, cracked egg,
The plates of your skull
Drift together and knit.

The apples circle above you.
You prove Copernicus wrong.
Little earth-beast, totem,

Your arms have the power.
You are the eighth.
They have waited
And they will obey.

There is no room for us.
In what strange universe
Have you taken your place?

The seven apples revolve.

We stand before you,
Two dark doors to our world,
Nothing more.

Nothing moves but our eyes;
They track you like cats.

Open us. Open us.

IV. Lightning Storm

SPAT

She picked up the diamond hammer
And smashed the ruby sink.

"See! See!," he shrieked,
"Look what you've done!
What will we drink?"

For answer, she struck
The bed's amethyst frame
With her pillow of jade.

He started flapping his elbows
Like two chicken wings.

"Aieeee! Fine!
There's nowhere to sleep!"

His fingers were muffling his ears.

For answer, she started
Shredding her silks,
A worm in reverse.

She stepped into the garbage pail
And hung it around her neck
With a ravelling string.

He peered through his fingers,
Grids or a grate.

"I'd like some honesty around here,"
She said,
Clattering down the garnet stairs.

She left him in a puddle
Of silver tears.

LIGHTNING STORM

All silver-stripe, cloud
Night long
The carpentering rain
Has been hammering at the house,

Quicksilver.
Now our turrets are glowing,
We are sealed up tight,
Ship-shape.

If there is a world
Beyond these windows of water
Streaming icicle-thick,
We don't know it.

If someone has taken
A razor, and slit the sky's
Tight sheet,
Causing this grey drape of water

Which falls like a waterfall
From a great cliff in China
We only know
We are safe on the one, solid

Grey shelf of stone.
For weeks now,
We have kept the precious message
Safe in the medicine chest

Where it tells us, tomorrow
The sky will be all blue, and electric,
The water green, white-foamed,
While our house slides silently

Off on its slow, easy float.
For weeks, we have been letting in
The doves who have fluttered their feathers
At our windows, and slept in pairs

At our doors.
And it will not be long now before
They begin to wake on their perches
And sing to the little oil pictures

Of the small waves leaping
In front of our porch like fish,
Flickering sometimes like leaves,
And take them to the houses

Of the people
Who think
They are still living on land.

HOUSEWIFE

What can be wrong
That some days I hug this house
About me like a shawl, and feel
Each window like a tatter in its skin,
Or worse, bright eyes I must not look through?

Now my husband stands above me
High as ever my father did
And I in that house of dolls, which,
When young I could not shrink to.

I feel the shrinkage in each bone.
No matter what I do, my two girls
Spoil like fruit. Already they push us back
Like too-full plates. They play with us
Like dolls.

The road before the house is like a wish
That stretches out and out and will not
Stop, and the smallest hills are built
Like steps to the slippery moon,
But I
Circle this lit house like any moth
And see each day open its fingers
To disclose the stone,—which hand, which hand?
And the stone in both.

Once, I drove my car into a tree.
The bottles in the back
Burst like bombs, tubular glass beasts,
Giving up the ghost. My husband
Thought it was the road. It was.
In the rearview mirror, it curved and curled,
Longer and stronger than the road ahead,
A question of perspective, I thought then.
I watched it until it turned, and I did not.
I sucked in pain like air,
As if, I, the rib, had cracked.

I did not feel this pain, not then,
Almost in my mouth. I wiggle this life
And find it loose. Like my girls,
I would pull it out, would watch
Something new and white
Push like mushrooms from the rich red soil.
But there is just this hole, this bone.

So I live inside my wedding ring,
Beneath its arch,
Multiplying the tables of my days,
Rehearsing the lessons of this dish, that sleeve,
Wanting the book that no one wrote,
Loving my husband, my children, my house,
With this pain in my jaw,
Wanting to go.

Do others feel like this? Where do they go?

THE FIRST MADAM

The skin,
A thin tissue of lies,
What goes over the skin
A thin tissue of silk,
Thin spider threads
Black widow spider threads
So many limbs.

I am the absolute virgin
A red light in black rooms
The red blood that never falls.
Never pierced
By the arms and the legs,
The shiny blue mucous cries.

More safe than a bank.
Men make their deposits.
The silver converted to ash.
The tiny silver ships
Dying like fish
On the smooth sheet of the shore.
Dying and rotting
The shore covered with them,
Dying, eyes out,
Bellies up.

Sometimes,
In a china robe
Controlling the spider threads
Of the globe.
This fleet will import.
This fleet will import children,
Perfectly white,
Their brains
Beginning to die
Before they are born.

The mother
Crying over the cot.
The mother
Offering her arm,
The good rape,
The silver needle goes in.
Now,
The man is buckling his pants.

Doors opening and closing
Like cards in a deck
The face cards my choice.
Stacked!

I will only have so many
Exist. That one will be emptied.
I am the blood light in black rooms
And I fill and empty people
Like ash trays.

THE PICTURE: WOLVES IN THE TREE*

For Bernard Hallote and Cynthia Ozick

In the picture,
Five white wolves sit in a tree.
The sixth has hidden himself
In the works of a grandfather clock.

They are afraid of being eaten,
But of course, this is what happens.
They are not really wolves,
But six wooly lambs.

They only pretend to be wolves.
The are afraid of the wolf.
They sit in a blasted tree
In a desolate snow-covered steppe.

They all stare straight ahead.
Blue pines are jagged behind them.
It is a mystery how they got up there.
It is a mystery how the wolf eats them.

They seem to be made of the snow
And are not very nourishing.
But still, they are eaten.
The sixth deserves our concern

Crouched stiffly and patiently
Under the pendulum and weights.
When is it safe to come out?
He thinks of his brothers

In the tree in the snow.
He thinks of the North Wind.
Puffing the face of the clock.
He wants to sneeze from the dust.

---

*The picture of the tree with five wolves was painted by one of Freud's most famous cases,
The Wolf Man.

There are two possible ends to his story.
In one, the constant tickings and chimings
Drive him quite mad.
The tickings turn slowly to snow.

He digs his way out,
Smears himself with butter,
And lies down on the hearth of the wolf.
He wears a little red hood for good measure.

The wolf is surprised,
But knows just what to do.

In the other,
He comes out, thinner but wiser,
Knows his pulse is a clock,
And goes to the market for wives.

He brings home a fat one.
He has fourteen children
And teaches them hopscotch
As he used to play it.

He makes a good living
Building grandfather clocks.
They are all big enough
For a fat sheep to sleep in.

He keeps a huge pot boiling
Under his chimney,
His house, of course,
Made of brick. At night,

His wife is often quite tired.
She takes off her apron
And asks what's it all for.
He says,

"The perpetuation of hopscotch,"
And turns on his side.
When he dies, the whole village
Calls him *The Sage*.

THE WHALE AND THE POLAR BEAR

*The whale and the polar bear, it has been said, cannot wage war on each other,
for since each is confined to his own element, they cannot meet.*

—SIGMUND FREUD

The whale and the polar bear
Met early one dawn
As the sun crept into the sky
Like lovely crab claws.

The polar bear had many harpoons.
He had heard tales from whalers.
The whale had a thick, slippery skin

And a spout which sent most of the ocean
Onto the floe.
"My aim is better," bragged the bear.
(In fact, he had a charley horse.)

"My head is cracking your ice,"
Bragged the whale, butting again.
(In fact, his head hurt.)
"You know," said the bear

Watching the whale,
"It is said we never may meet."
"How can that be?" asked the whale

Whose head thudded,
And whose eyes were quite crossed.
The bear told him the tale.
"Elemental," laughed the whale.

Their wars are now passed in jokes
At the tellers of tales.
Of late, the bear
Sits at the edge of the sea

And daily, the whale swims by
With his greetings, which lately
Take the form of fresh fish.
The bear, who has sharp claws,

Takes the whale's barnacles
Off with a flick.
Today, the whale recalled bears
Are strong swimmers too,

And the bear, as bears will do,
Remembered his aunt telling him of a whale
Who had once been found on the ice
Which there, they call *land*.

They never make war, and,
Although occasionally,
They toy with attacks on the men
Who sail by in boats

Nothing has come of it yet.
But often, the whale swims around ships
With the bear and his cubs
On his back.

POSTHUMOUS POEM

The sun reaches out with its hot hands,
Touching everything,
And what it will not buy, it burns.
We hide in the dark house,
But the blinds' sharp shadows
Cut into our safety
As precisely as knives.

At night, the sun sinks into water,
Releasing its inks,
Filling the valley like a dark cup
It forces up to its lips.

Sometimes, the sun bruises the sky
To purple and black, puffing and swelling with clouds.

Then the stones of our graves
Wait like an army,
Hungry and wet,
At the gates of the town.

The quick peer through the spiked bars,
Throwing rocks at our names.
Even the dead
Live far from safety.

Late at night, the sky splits
And our names say where we are.
Anyone can find us.
Only the wrong ones will.

We are the haunted.
White ones stand above us
Where we are dark in our skins.

They leave us their questions,
Their pasts, and their cries.
They grow like weeds on our graves,
Choking the clover,

And we cannot speak
When the sky splits above us,
Pushing its bad dreams out.

V. Immortalities

ELEGY FOR SYLVIA PLATH

You are the kite
That searches and floats; the cloud
Forming a pupil in the eye
Of the sky
You have been everywhere, looked
Everywhere,
Once, twice,
There is still
Some gold sand cold
In your shoe; there are still
Some coins with strange faces
You never can spend

Now you are running
Faster and faster,
Trying to stay on;
The earth is only
A great colored globe
The ones you want
Are just over the curve
Crouched down
Their fingertips showing over
The horizon like stones,
Their soft hair
Tangled
Like trees

O they turn with the earth
And you turn with it too.
The whole world is turning
Under its stones.
You never will reach them.
You can't, and you won't.

II.

Finally, you come to a field
Sunk in the hills, empty and plain.
The grass is graying and sparse.
The sun is going down
Like a blue hand of veins
Holding a match.
It touches the hills.
They ignite to a great fiery ring.
You make your way forward,
Your hand over your eyes,
And you can see the bones of your hand;
They are orange.

On the horizon are trees,
Many of them, black as burned wood.
The sun goes down, softly,
In jerks,
As if drawn in by a breath.

They are not trees.
They are the family you sought,
Like Puritans,
Dressed in dead black.
Now the sun is edging them
With reddish-gold gilt;
And it flares up once more,
Burning its last.
You go and stand with them in the fire.

III.

Sylvia, I opened the magazine,
And there it was, your poem,
Your name at the bottom,
All those letters, eleven of them,
Standing up like good soldiers,
As if there had been
No war, no battle,
And no one had ever died.

Well, *it* was alive,
And you, you had to be sitting somewhere,
On the edge of a bed,
Licking a stamp,
Thinking the bitter thoughts,
Shaking in your herbs of words,
Closing a window, sniffing for gas,
Hearing again
The grim ringing of phones.

Yes, it's bad.
But somewhere
You are holding on
To a ledge with your nails.
Hang on.
Keep picking at the rope
Tying you to the tracks.
Remember the dark days,
The cold, the snow
Peeling from the sky
In thin icy veils,
The hard-boiled eggs hot from the pot
Held by wool mittens
To keep small hands warm.

Hold on.
We are adding a room to the house.
We are fattening its ribs.
We will paint the walls pink.
There will be flowers and lamps.
It seems, when the sun sets,
You are diminished to a cry.
God, but you have grown so little and frail!

There were red veins in the sky.
Now the sky has bled itself white.
Our own blood is thin.
The earth turns one cheek, then another,
Spins,
Spins you away.

[55]

TO SOMEONE WHO WAS NEVER UNHAPPY, OR AFRAID

Now you walk only at night
When fog thickens the air
As memory or dreams.
So perhaps you were wrong then,
Wrong all along.
Each word gone, each word
Had its arms, its legs, its little shout.
You abandoned them on cliffs
Like the Chinese,
Those six-toed thoughts,
Those with none.

You were wiser as a child.
You kept your doll with pits for eyes.
You wondered what she saw
Until you saw. And your doll
With hair turned green by the Tintex box
That should have turned it brown,
You kept and loved,
And sometimes, late, your own hair
Turned seaweed green and floated loose
Like sand on blue black tides of air.

What did you fear?
You were so quiet, like a doll.
Was it love's little country
Behind plain fabric, decent, like curtains
On other people's windows—
What people did to one another there?
You could not hear them
Through the long planks of the floor
Covering like coffin tops.

The lighted rooms beneath,

The words
Melted like wax, grotesque,
The sun's injury; you muffled them
In earth, its bandage, rich, rich
And dark.
So you mended love's fabric.
You stopped your ears.
And this took time,
Took years.

And now it is not even clear
Whether you live here,
Or are a guest.
You walk only at night
Through dreams or fog.
You wonder what went wrong.

There is propriety here,
And much quiet.
The sky is bluer than a children's book.
And order is soothing, like sweet tea, or a drug.
The neighborhood is good,
And each small granite house
Boasts its carved angel or stone saint.
At night, all lights are out.

You cannot see, but sometimes
A new guest is driven
To the gate, over the threshold, down
The gravelly path, is set down
Like a long black stone in a plain old brooch
Her relatives ring about, black pearls,
Before they all file out,

And it is strange how the one thing
Their fingers long to touch
Is not a flower on the wreath, so neat,
But the one fallen to the grass, half lost,
Or the lone dandelion, gone to seed,
Nodding its frowsy curlered head
Above its housedress, raggy, bottly green,
While inside its box, the well-dressed doll

Is curled, is splendid
As a Christmas toy, lies both eyes shut,
And when the box tilts up
Before earth's cellar doors
(which only close and close)
Will not wake up
But with the first strike of the spade
Its jaw begins to move, clack, clack,

A marionette's jaw, so fast;
This is desperate, this is the last,
I must tell you this, and this,
It shouts and shouts,
But the relatives are mending love's fabric,
Are turning round, are turning back,
And cannot hear
What it cannot speak.

IMMORTALITIES

I enter the arena
Of detergents,
Of the white smile
The preserved face
Embalmed in its cream.

A slight difference
The grey wrinkles of the mind;
A slight difference
The greyness of the womb
The square shape of its babies
The silent sound of their cries

The major difference
Their price tags
The major difference
The bracelet of letters
Neither pink nor blue
Spelling your own name.

It is a horror:
They will buy them
Uncurl
Their black tendril vines
From your flesh ones
So you are for sale
So you are judged.
The more pregnant your shelves
The more valuable

Good
Brood mare of the mind.

You enter
The world of housewives
The checked dresses
They filled again and again
Money
Saved in a sack.
The busts of marble generations
Nod and nod. Wife,

Mathematical miracle,
Worth nothing at all,
Multiplied, all.
And so she grows bitter
On the juice of her belly,
Monstrous lemon
Swallowed down whole.
And so the author grows bitter
On his books
Their corners protruding,
Four painful horns.

This is the time of the something else:
Elizabeth sees her;
She forms in ice crystals
Behind violet eyes; Marilyn saw her,
Always cold; and Sylvia saw her

Standing on a corner in air,
Selling her wares—
The little match girl
With nothing to sell

But herself

Crying *buy it, buy it*

In the worst wind
Crouched to ignite
The tiny blue flame.
Not much, not much at all.
She had no fire
For the hem of her dress,
No spectacular thing

Just her thin blue blood
And her tiny sparks into flame
No one would strike
With frozen lips saying

It all comes to this,
To this,
I am always here inside,
Inside everyone,

Cold, the child, the only child,
And though the prince
Rides by with the gold globe
On his knees like the sun
I don't want it

His eyes are covered
By splinters of ice

He cannot see
They cannot see
Nor could I

And his hooves struck the stones to tinder
As, small match,
She wavered and went out

With each new birth.
And each new death.

VI. Sleeplust

INVALID

Sitting stiller
Than a stopped heart
I remember
The pink candy hearts,

The raised words,
I Love You,
How they went down,
Smoothly
Swallowing love.

I remember
When life dissolved:
People, high heels,
Aspirin in water,
A mist
The sun burned away.

Now,
My pink pills.
I hoard them,
Count them,
Sweet
Pink abacus of health.

I let
Each one lie
On my tongue.
The sugar dissolves.
O round world,
Universe seed

Nails
The shutter over
The hole
In the heart,
Stops the black draft;
Patches the plaster
Of bones,
Bicycle-patches the lungs.
I can breathe.

The others
Rattle and flutter
In their jars,
Like heartbeats,
Uncountable,
And from them
Invisible veins.

They are lamps.
When night drops
Like a drug mask
I visit them on their shelves.
Heads of pins,
The angels within
In their shifts,
Slits cut for wings.

Lover of bending,
Breath,
I live
In the suicide's house.
How the body flicks on
The gas jets,
Hangs bodies, swollen
To swing
From the beams.

The tiny pink pills
Grow thin hands
In the blood,
Taking them down,
Turning them off,
Unraveling to thread
The cloud
That would stopper
The heart.

I survive.
Miser of medicines,
I survive,
Melting ice
Into air,
Curtaining gallows
Of ribs,
Fixing my eye
On the ground
For the loose tile,
The fall,
While

The sun's
After-image, black,
Burns its way through,
Red-globe,
Into blood-light.

LADY WITH CUT FLOWERS

Your gold key turns in the lock,
And the tumblers are magnetic,
Are golden, let you silently in.

In the entrance hall,
A mirror, fit for museums,
Holds your face

Like two Italian, tapering hands.
Lady of porcelain skin, ebony hair.
Some forsythia petals have fallen

From the great vase,
Like the gold clothes of angels
Who dressed in a hurry, then left,

Secure in their maids.
Your beautiful face is a painting
You have painted yourself,

Master, and like her, your smile, ambiguous.
You circle among the ivories and ebonies,
Then stop. Outside, the pigeon flies

A perfect circle
Under the perfect circle of the gold sun
Your key has opened.

Bach circles perfectly in your air,
Your gold dust, his notes, precious.
Mother of miracles!

It happened somehow.
Your white dogwood skin?
Was it that belly, its perfect red jewel?

Yours, faceted as a ruby
And more valuable by far?
Mother of dynasties.

Thin hands lifting the silver
With Chinese blue veins.
Inside, lined with red, like a carpet,

Oriental, calling Agamemnon in,
More valuable with age.
A kind of a legend.

Is that it?

And your black hair that spreads
Like a silk fan, the blue threads,
The purple. Others have grey.

And the envy of others!
So you keep your shades drawn,
The claw hands, nails filthy,

Constantly scaling your glass.
Lady, you say to yourself, *lady*.
It is a life, it is a life.

Delhi and Paris,
And the sphinxes, who run through
Your dreams wearing your jewels

And the pyramids under water,
Surfacing in the night as your vaults.
And the people in them who unwind
Themselves, and speak to you and speak

To you, sadly, sadly.
And your husband, in the wall,
A locked safe to which you alone

Own the combination you never forget.
The hours are covering you,
Tanzanites;

The hours are reaching your lips;
Already they have stopped up your ears.
The thick carpet has swallowed all

Footsteps and strung them together
Like pearls. Under their weight,
Your tulip neck bends, bends down.

So there are no tracks.
The tracks on the kitchen wall
Showing your sons' heights, a sin,

Immediately painted—the lives
Sheeted by paint. It is clean.
The perfection of white walls,

And rice walls. Now do you think
They would have to chop you down
Like a tree to find the rings

Which would prove you have lived?
Your fingers moving nervously
Among the yellow petals,

Your other hand holding your bouquet of flowers,
Pink peonies, yellow roses, babies' breath,
Dogwood,

Thinking, more beautiful than anything,
More beautiful than the most beautiful,
The most beautiful,
Well-kept grave.

THE GRANITE LADY OF VERMONT

For Mrs. Mary Ecroyd Hinkle and Mr. C. H. Gale

On perfect days, if you sit just right in the niche
Of the jagged pocked boulder jutting into the river
And feel with your fingers for the rough piece of stone
That dents in, shaped like a quarter,
And then look two inches to the right

You can see her face

The perfect face of a medieval lady
Her head turned to the side and into her cowl
While her robes seem to billow
As the water laps over
And she dreams her sad dream

Taking no notice of storms and of tides;
And at the river, which seems the fuse of it all—
Gold lying on the rocks, and under the water,
And the water a surface of silver, the water
The pigment for the great dyes of Persia,

And the leaves
Covered with letters, and hieroglyphs, and runes—
It is not hard to believe
She will gain the dimension
She needs again for her breathing

That she will lift her head
Up from the rock like a pillow
And into the air, growing suddenly life size,
And before she leaves,
Or turns her cheek back into the granite,

Patiently tell you all she has seen.

Patron saint of the state
For whom the trees fling down their leaves,
Their gloves of orange and scarlet each autumn,
For whom they draw them on again in the spring
With their delicate tracings, once more gone green.

She knows why the flood had undone
The frogs who lived on the dry banks of mud,
Now gone under, like swimmers who stayed out too long,
And why, when the rain comes down at an angle,
The toads cross the road like animal leaves,

Some hitting the wheels, some getting across.
It is the state, it is the state,
Held by some spell under the great bell of time.

She will remind you
How you took a friend to the train, crying tears
From your belly, saying, someone is leaving, always
Someone is leaving;
She will say, see,

The leaves are getting ready for their trip
They are going together; those who stay behind
Will watch the last blow across the road,
Then they go after
And the flowers are folding themselves up

Like clothes in the tiny cupboards of grass
Going up in the pure flame, invisible.
And you tell her,
I will not have this woman die
Who took children to Switzerland

When their fathers hung themselves in bathrooms
With ebony floors and chandeliers of crystal,
And came down a mountain in a Model T Ford
And its wheels went over the edge, spinning,
And all the people in the bus passing

Screamed for their lives
And the curves were all hairpins
And not one of hers moved.
And I will not have this man die
Who hunted to eat on these very mountains

And remembers today,
As if he just came in from the snow,
The friend who was killed by the bear,
He got the deer but the bear got him.
One day, he went up the mountain, and shot him,

And propped his gun against a tree in the snow
And because it was snowing
A piece of bark over the muzzle
So no water would enter
And went down with his knife to finish him off.

But the bear, waking,
Grabbed him, and hugged him,
And threw him against a tree, over and over,
And the doctor said later
His intestines were all mixed in

With his vital organs, so squeezed he was
And it took his three brothers and their friends
Three days to track his body and find it
Where it lay, sleeping, quiet, one drop of blood
On his cheek in the snow.

And she says,
Remember, you cut your knuckle when you cut the onion
And, round as a world
It was undone without any fuss
And you finished your job without any fuss

But you cried from its juice
And she says, remember
How you swam the pathway of sun down the water
Thinking, swimming the pathway of sun is so easy,
Until a cloud covered the sun

And the gold world was sunken
And when you turned back,
The vision had drowned, and gone under,
And now you see yourself in the water
As you sit on the rock

Drying out and browning
Like this very same leaf
And the blue drop of water you held in your hand
Like a world
Is entirely gone.

FOR A HAPPY MARRIAGE
Charles and Charlotte Mitchell

I.

They are folding up the house
Like a carton.
They fold it with care.
They wrap all their things
And put them inside.
They wrap a glass figure of their bodies
And put it inside.
The men driving the truck nod
And drive off.
They are left standing in the dust,
Holding hands.
The last thing they see is the carton:
It leaves like a special delivery letter.
They do not know its address.

II.

They live in deep country,
Between five maples, in front of a brook.
The thirty-five years were sentries.
Only one of them fell.

You wonder: what did they think?
What do they do? Then
The door swings open: ordinary.
Photographs of grandchildren.
There, it is ordinary
For people to step from their pictures
And take a tour of the house.

His great love for clocks.
How their hearts give up, like small bees.
The room fills with ticks, swarming.
He comes to the hives unprotected,
And never is stung.

Time himself rests in that room.
He sleeps in one clock, then another.

"I've had thirteen majors."
He means operations.

She has hair blued by the moon.
She collects silver bells and brass bells.
They strike like gongs with handles of dragons;
They all call to things.
She calls them and sees them.
He scours the hill houses
Looking for more.

She is proper and sweet
And necessary as the Mayflower.
Her blue veins collapse,
Sinking and hard.
She is dying more quickly
Than a world can imagine.
"I wanted to lose weight, but not this way."

Now he remembers the years as they went.
Now he counts up:
"She never liked fishing.
She was on the wrong side always.
A rainbow trout jumped at her shoelace.
Later, I caught him, or one just like."

The mountains are blue,
And their mist is rising.
She is water sinking into the earth.
Her hair is still done on Mondays.
Soon
The woman will come to her home.

Her husband cries before strangers
And is not ashamed.
"You keep her comfortable, keep busy,
And forget when you can."
More and more, he remembers.

III.

Now she is dead,
The truck drives her away.
She sits in the front seat
On her husband's invisible lap.
Her four sisters swoop round like swallows,
Their faces cat faces,
With white feathers for whiskers.
They follow the truck as far as they can.
Eventually, they lose it in a thick
Dust of petals.
The driver stops for every light
And every sign and sharp turn.
He drives the old truck sedately.
They hug each other and laugh
As, slowly, he takes the turn over the horizon
And they drive on in the air.
The man driving is steady.
He once drove a school bus.
They go slowly and sweetly.
They will set up shop when they come.

WIDOW

I am dead.
That is the only difference,
That the others can no longer hear me.

In couples, in black,
They leave the green lawn.
My husband is smiling,
A wife on his arm.

Not yet.
Her white dress is still
Only a cloud.
She stitches it together
With her sweet clever words.
They fall over her marble slab teeth

Like children,
Like children.

I stand in front of them
Like a roadblock. My mother, my father,
Slightly surprised.
They are dressed entirely in ivy.
It grows from the earth of their bodies.

So they have put me to bed.
They are good: they bring drinks of water
To the flowers, the bright hungry mouths.
They are sensible, will not

Bang their heads on the tiles of the floor.
I follow
Down the long road in a kind of a dust.
The cars wait.

What was it I wanted to see?
Why did I want to see it?
Everything spinning, the continent top.

I have shouted into the mouths of geranium horns.
No sound.
Their stems turned more green,
Or else withered.

Even the pennies on my eyes
When I put them back
More transparent than air.

VALENTINE FROM THE SUN

This is the year of the heart.
Now it is turning on us like a tiger.

It is counting the beads of our blood
In the strings of our veins.

It has touched them; it knows them all.
We have collected these heads,

Like cannibals, on stakes.
They hang in the bare trees

Like lanterns or apples.
At nightfall, they all start to talk.

They are confessing their sins, and ours.
Above, the moon is nodding its head.

The moon is pronouncing its sentence
Like a priest deaf or mad.

It is drawing a cloud across its face
Like a sleeve. The wind is laughing,

And the dead leaves are running.
Our prayers are burrowing in the earth

Like moles. Our dreams are sprouting
Arms from their eyes like potatoes.

We want to take root,
But the sun is coming up,

Angry as any god.
He is flooding the earth like light.

He is beating in the sky
Like a terrible heart.

The air is burning like blood
With a fever. The fields of the earth

Are blushing, and the hot hands of the heat
Are digging us up. We are clinging

Like leaves to the dry hands of our mothers,
But the tree hands can hold us

For only one season.
They have disinherited us,

And now we are blowing over the big roads,
The black lanes of tar, and the cars

Are stringing the highways
Like mechanical cats, their breath

Foggy and warm. A few get across,
Pointing up to the sun, the hot eye

Of the storm.

PAST

For Michael Denneny

On pale days,
The curving landscape
A sheet of rice paper,

Thin,
Its trees
Brushstrokes in waters,
Slowly, it curls into a shape

Like a morning glory,
Fluted horn,
Then its tunes
Are the tunes of yesterday;

Today's melody thins,
And goes out

Old faces will shimmer
Just under the new ones,
Rising,
Just under
The thin skin of a lake.

Hypnotic, new hands
Move in the old gloves;
Filmy women come in long dresses

Office fans revolve in their hair,
The soft buzz of flies, fine dust
A gold heat, a haze:

When did the smooth carbon road
Become the copy?
When did the rutted road
Seize your foot,
Dragging you back?

Now the dark shelves
Of eight-day clocks
Give up the time they have kept
To themselves, chiming a song

Madly familiar
The dear ones, they are back;
Their faces are not graves—
The faces that tangle
In a gold ivy of curls

So maddeningly familiar
Your tongue gropes thickly
In honey, for the twin tablets,
The lost, graven words.

THE LOST DAY

This is the day someone forgot.
It has ragged edges,
A piece of paper torn out.

Perhaps in the corner
A bit of scribbling.
Or a smudge in the sky,

Like a cloud.
Impressions from the pen
Of the day that just ended.

It is a white day.
It has white trees with white leaves.
It has a thick dust falling.

It has white bedrooms
Where everything is covered
In tight grains of frost.

The white hands
Of the seven-day clock
Are burrowing back into the two

Deep holes for the key.
Nothing chimes.
You remember your husband's pulse.

It winds down like a clock.
Someone's eyes are fixed
On the white clock.

Two more minutes to the needle of snow.
Your mother lies on her bed, rails up.
You lie on your bed.

Your hands
Pull your two eyelids down.
Tomorrow,

Life will blare like a radio
When the current goes on.
The sun will remember

And open your eyes
With its two thin gold needles,
Its hands.

SLEEPING IN THE ROOM OF A DEAD CHILD

For Richard Booth

The furniture, of course, has been changed.
Yet the room waits,
The vanity with its curved arms,

Its triple mirror,
Holds your full face
And your half face, and your half face again.

The three of you wait.
The moon in the sky
Has broken in half.

Into black space, it stares.
The high round window, like a porthole,
Steers the wind wildly

Through thickening trees,
Becalming itself.
The old bed is beautiful and plain

As a marriage.
Its sheets have stretched tight
With the wait, tight white skin.

It is not far down the hall.
The mother and father
Lie locked in their dreams,

Two drowned swimmers
Who tried for the air.
She says, there is nothing to finish.

She plucks the hands
From the faces of clocks,
Watches and clocks,

The huge hands of the moon.
Her thin hands
Release them in space.

They strike on the stars.
In her sleep, she smiles,
Then sighs.

There is nothing
He wants to begin.
He is looking for booths

With the tickets to last year
When all the towns
Smiled from their steeples

When the train
Made unscheduled stops
In towns which never were there.

The braking train wheels
Set the clockwork in motion.
A new country begins.

They move together in sleep,
Her entangling hair
Wrapping them,

Seaweed, the ship ribs
Settling with the tide.
What have they not seen?

His death
Was a white dot
At the end of the tunnel

Clock face
Smashing them all,
Then a world, glaring white.

So they sleep.
The room does not sleep.
It preserves its memories,

A yearbook, a number of books
Showing a taste.
The bed calls,

The vanity prepares you,
And you will get in
But first, there is a place in the center

Light rays intersecting,
Planks intersecting,

Tiny clocks from your eyes
Like pure acid,
Eating your cheeks.

And then you are forced in,
Prepared by the vanity,
Between the white sheets

Beneath the tight covers
Baptized in half-light
Held by its arms

Unwilling,
And willing,
Anonymous bride.

SLEEPING IN THE COUNTRY

Sleeping in the country
I am sure

That the bed will fold
Me over like the two white shells
Of a clam

That the moon
Will develop in the sky
Like a pearl

That the green heads
Of trees
Will bow over the house

Like grandmothers
That the covers of books
Will open

And the pastel animals
Run loose in the woods
That the cat

Will write in his diary
Dipping his whisker
In ink

That the stars
Will stroll through the sky
Doing their shopping

That the brook
Will erase the mistakes
Of the bank

That the fish
Will rise up on their tails
And sing to the owl

Until he is blinded
With joy,
That the mice

Will grow antlers
And run in the moonlight
In herds

That the four-chambered rocks
Will know themselves
Pulsing with blood

That the sun
Is behind a curtain
Smiling

And will rise
In the morning

Palming it all
Like a great golden mole

The day in his teeth
Like a jewel.

MONKS

It is no small thing to wake up
And find tiny brown monks
Suspended from the branches of pines

Singing their hymns
Chanting their orisons
Tapping their bells,

Fastened to fingertips, together;
But when they turn away,
Showing only their brown backs,

Looking like oak leaves, wrinkled,
Blown into the wrong trees
Falling into silence

As into deep centuries
The only sound the green wind of time:
It is that

Their slight revolution, a half-turn,
The moon turning its dark side,
It is that

The great, the unacceptable thing.

WINTER NIGHT

Under the thick carpet of snow
And under the hill
There is much activity.

Down deep, the rooms
Are full of windows
Which are mirrors,

Doubling everything.
The hoarded nuts multiply,
The sleeping moles too.

There are visits by the long
Low white ones who are sleek
To the dark houses

Which are long and polished
And lie flat.
Their teeth open windows

Just over the eyes.
The faces that come
Are full of fur and kindness.

They are warm, and have soft paws.
They make strange motions.
Above, the snow falls,

Silent,
Below, with the sound of stones.
This is how heaven begins.

SLEEPLUST

In the room, the bed hums
Like an expensive car or a cab.
How expensive, the meter of days,

How expensive,
The blink of the lids,
The nickels, the dimes,
The great cost.

It waits like a great chauffeur
At the beautiful blue curb,
The day's end.
It is everything.

You get in, peaceable fossil
Pressed between sheets,
Stopped. The roof comes down close,
Holds, wool, to your form.

You have come down the twenty-four
Stone steps to this well.
The blue dark floats you like water.
Your ancestor floats by, a shell,
The sound of the sea in her ear,

Beached.
Ghost ships go by, whispering plans.
Through the window's pale eye
Slip white spars

Shattering nothing.
You dismember the clocks,
Wind on their springs like rings
And, gold lady of time,

Gold bell on each breast.
Smashed clock faces
Sliver your sheets,
A kind of a snow. The window fills,

The last stone, sealing the tomb.
Veins of your hand, Rosetta-stoned.
Miles above, excavations begin.
The time shaft sinks

From the earth rim
Wanting you, at its center.
Grains of sand gather around you,
Cushions, preserving, embalmed.

The bed travels smoothly,
Without jolt.
Your blood chimes the hours;
There are no hours.

Once, in past centuries,
You lay down,
Turned on your side.

MADNESS

The trees have taken back their benediction.
As I watch, they lift their arms up,
Plugging into the sockets of stars.
A faint hum is heard; it deepens, like water.
Dark shapes appear at the rim of the woods.
Their eyes glint yellow in the light
Though there is no light.

Safety is the charmed circle of breath;
Inside the room, it forms in puffs,
The house grown cold as an ice house.
The feet stall; the heart is a battery,
Wearing down. One by one,

The planks of the walls withdraw;
They recede, turning to trees, dark leaves.
The roof lifts off as a cloud.
The starling who lent his wings for arms
To the kitchen clock flies off,
Leaving a hole, as if for a moon,
A hole in the ice, solid ice beneath.

This is how it ends, then,
Toes curled in the grass, no roof,
Because a switch has been thrown;
The moon sailing down the sky
Like a ship without sails, going dark,

The breath, a circle of moths
Eating this, my last dress,
And my bones, crackling tubes,
Trying to carry the tune
Hummed by minds the size of walnuts,
Razor eyes, the minds
Behind the yellow, electrified eyes.

SUICIDE

The drama of suicides, then?
Your own body, eternal and white,
Marble-sleeping and white.

The others who carved you
Around you perpetually
Their heads bent down

Like flowers, like flowers
Under a hail of reproaches
The angels who loved you

Buzzing around them like wasps
Tiny mouths, wasp-size
Biting into their ears

With their twin rows of teeth
Holding on, little earrings
Whispering *reproaches, reproaches.*

White as marble, as snow
You are the first frost
You are the killing frost

They fall across your body

Like lilies
Like lilacs
Like roses

They are planted in cursed ground
Every leaf they bear
Accuses, accuses

And no one will ever forget.

No wonder you cross your arms
Over your breast
No wonder you cover your nipples

Twin tiny snakes gone back
Into their white beds of earth.
You are white.

You are inside of the apple,
Innocent, innocent.
Their teeth

Turn in their mouths;
Their tongue is an animal
Cowering.

You bring them the taste of the earth.

II.

Death is only a commuter
Hanging on by the strap
In the heat;

His knuckles show white
His brief case beneath him
Packed up with papers

Dog-eared and grey.
He has called on them all
The housewife doing her cleaning,

Her hair tied in a cloth
The lovers wrapped in their sweat
A thin tissue of silk

They have slammed the door
On his foot;
See how misshapen.

They have slammed the hospital
Hard in his face, the cartilaginous nose.
He is pitiable, pitiable.

Most everyone knows him.
He does not deal in asps.
He is a hard worker, tireless.

III.

First, you bought them
And they were numbered,
Six digits at least.

One in a series of breaths
Spiked on a file
Your name on the label

Probably misspelled.
Did you have the right change?
Whose hands held them last?

In your hands,
Germs ate at the faces of coins.
Then you walked back.

The maniac on the block
Let you pass by
Without even a glance.

You turned the key in the lock.
You saw its halo of smudges.
You walked in.

The stale air caught its breath.
The pictures had nothing to say,
Having said it before.

Despondent, the cushions sagged deeper,
As if borne down by bone.
You put the bottle in the center,

A tiny bouquet.
It blooms so fast now
Its flowers are black,

Black and misshapen,
Mushrooms, or fungi.
You take a glass from the shelf.

It is not really clean.
You fill it with water.
The water is old;

It has been through your body
Before; it has been over rock
It has worn rock into sand

You will drink it once more
You are turning to sand.
The arched neck of the faucet

Turns away, old nurse, indifferent.
She has seen this before.
The sink skin is mottled with age,

Has grown a grate over its throat.
You swallow them, one at a time.
Heaviness steals one limb at a time.

Your mind begins its race
Around the room like a rat.
The glasses watch from their shelf.

The silver stares from its shelf.
Silent anonymous accomplices,
They watch, grey as clerks,

Serviceable,
The bottle is knocked over
You are knocked over

Your hair is oily
Your eyes are open
You are grey and hard as a stick.

Sometime later, they come
The jelly glasses give their report,
Insignificant country

You have fallen.
The knives cut in here.
Things will remain as they were

For a generation at least.
They file out to the tune
Of "Rebuilding a Life."

Your small grey house is complete.

Impatient, the glasses

Stir on the shelves.
Impatient, the spoons
Stare at the doorway like eyes.

IV.

In silver and gold
In ruby and jet
In purl and crimson

Cleopatra took her life
From a great golden tray.
She was attended, gorgeous in silk.

She was a tapestry,
Her death the last golden thread.
When she pressed an asp to each breast

The eyes of the world
Swung to the east
Were blinded by purple and black.

Antony's silver sword
Was rubied with blood.
The sphinxes extended their claws.

All the gold grains
Fell through the gold glass
Like sand.

Each dune sighed like a sea.
The pyramids shifted their stones.
Heat stuck the chariots

To the great roads like glue.
Her face laughed
In the Romans' great shields.

Antony's hand gripped everyone's sword.
It was never to end.
They took up their reign

In the pillars of clouds.
Redder than sunsets, gold tinged,
They follow the armies of earth

Victorious as gold.

v.

On the screen,
Marilyn is soft as a cloud
Elizabeth is soft as a cloud

The dreamers are regimented in rows
Their dreams
Meeting overhead in smoke,

Kissing in clouds.
The floor is a hard granite field
Planted with popcorn

It never will reap.
A rat crosses a stockinged foot
Elizabeth's face

Marilyn's face
The girl feels the body's grey weight
She makes a mistake

She feels a tug at her heart
She grasps the hand of her lover
Sitting beside,

She clasps down on it,
Hard.

AGE

I grow old in the house of my body.
Wicker rockers tilt in my eyes.

Pink camellias grow in my hair
Though I clip them and clip them

They are whispering to my pleated breasts
And my thighs, you are *young, young, young.*

THE PHOTOGRAPH

If a woman looks at you
Long enough from a photograph

She understands all there is.

Her hands, hidden in the picture,
Trace the print of your fingers,
Draw your cardiac line.

She loses interest in her own hand.

She has spent years
In a drawer or an album.
If she was folded,
Her face has been scarred.

She is full
Of vengeance and wickedness.
She knows who she loves,
And she needs many transfusions.

Who is to say where her soul goes?
Her eyes
Follow you through the house, sly,
Behind the hangings, the lamps.

In spite of this,
She will never hurt you.
She studies your pictures,
Filling a book.

She moves back,
Vampire faced with massed crosses.
It happens like this:

You reach down to the picture,
Lifting her out.
Sick baby, she sticks.
The blanket hardens to wood.

At that instant,
Your palmprint changes to hers.

TRANSITIONS

Old.
Some kind of blight
Is eating the blooms of the walls.

Ants are crawling over
The gold face of the sun.

Now that you can see through trees,
It is clear the sap
Is a green worm which grows
Until it sees precisely what it wants,

Then stops.

Your body rests in a square
Of gelatinous air, a fancy French fish.
When a door slams,
Your air quivers, then rests.

No one comes near you, not close.
You are a blue country of veins,
A map everyone has left.

Now that you are learning to see this,
Learning the perfect quiet,
Someone else, very small, blood covered,

Is bawling, eyes sealed,
Quite blind,

But seeing the same things
He will forget as soon
As you have entirely left.

HOW IT HAPPENS

The miseries pile up at our door
Like mail for careless vacationers
And they are getting more clever
In the way they importune us

Sending them disguised as children selling mints
Or tulip bulbs in old boxes.
The tulips wilt together with the children.
We stay inside.

Circus masters, we stay inside.
Our miseries trained like lions
To impersonate chairs,
The glass that would have at our wrists

Forced into the disc of a dish.
In our three-ring rooms, we perform
Undeceived, safe,
Absorbed in our own withering.

EXIT

Some day, I shall walk out of this, as out of a house.
The door will slam, and the house will fall over
Like a prop, and the sky will spring into place
As if hinged: the street will go straight on
Through the cities, and into the desert, and we will live
There with our figs and our camels and our skins of old gold.
The sky will be clean, like clean glass.
The heat will shimmer in the air like soft satin.
It will be easy, like mailing a letter at the corner.

Now it is winter, and the sky is so thin
The dark is seeping through it already, like wet underpaint.
The windows are thick and dusty and heavy with bars.
The bannisters are round and the furniture is massive.
I am two-dimensioned and light, a pencil cartoon.
Now there is no way to get out but to go to the fire
And go up the chimney in smoke. Others are doing it.
Overhead, the night sky is heavy with crowds.

RECUPERATION

My room has become my hospital room.
My only visitors are the cats.

They come in one at a time.
None of them stays too long.

All day, my nurse, my green tree
Flutters its balinesque hands
In the motions of a sophisticated dance.

It stands up straight.
Underneath, are the brown bones of twigs.
It shows me what has to be done.

FORTUNE COOKIES

When the mind is most empty
It is most full.

Life as a fortune cookie.

Shaped like a bunting,
The destiny inside,
Four in a cellophane pack,
A family of sorts.

Will he see the pagoda
On top of the hill,
The forest fire in flames,
The leaves changing in autumn?

Omens? Auguries? Mere weather?

To take a message from a fortune
                           cookie
Is a delicate business.
To replace it with one of your own,
Far far worse.

So much do we know
Of fullness and emptiness.
So much do we affect one another.

VII. The Bridge

THE BRIDGE

When the bridge snapped
Like a dry plank
Jagged edges tilting down

The train hung
Like a thread
Like a necklace
Of rust

The two last cars
Holding on to the snapped track
Like teeth

Swaying over the water
As
Those green worms of summer
Sway from the leaves
Or the branches of trees

Then
Trusting the thread
Practically invisible
Except in bright light

Launching themselves
Seeming to float
Down to the grass

So the train
Let go,
A serpentine diving
Splintering the quiltwork of silver
And leaving no scar

Immediately creating

Square rooms full of embryos
Dressed up like grown people
And some
Embryos within embryos

Creating
A hurricane of compacts
Like twenty-dollar gold pieces

Sequins of loose change
Hats floating
Like flowers
Papers rising up, Japanese petals
Cast on pond waters

And lipsticks that slid
Back and forth like gold bullets
And cigars in their cases

Silver bullets
For the black hearts of werewolves

And all making
The same mazy motions
A ballet of hands
That had lost this and that

While on shore
There was quite a stir
But beneath
Fish pressed their faces

To the square panes of glass,
Each air bubble a world,
Rising up,
Effortless,

The mysterious, amazed faces
Of fish.

INDIAN CHIEF

I live in the absolute certainty of complete mystery.
There is the wind in the trees; it will stay there.
There is the water in the sea; it will remain.

There is the grain, the gourds, the maize.
They will stay, though, in spite of their roots
They are like wandering tribes who will not come

Every season. We have the seeds.
They are only partly complete;
The clouds have the rest, but in their wisdom

Save them for the great years. Now come the dry ones.
The parched earth that will not even take the print
Of the sharp foot of the deer, the splayed foot

Of the bear. We become dry mouths.
We resemble our feathers. The sun war-paints our faces,
The sun tomahawks our scalps, the moon, mirage of water,

While the leaves crackle in full summer, not whisper.
There is the rain dance, there is the witch doctor,
The visions, the chants, something to hold to

Like the neck of a horse. I have heard the war cries,
The breathing in back of the hills,
The terrible rush of horses melted to men,

The skull-bowls, the brain pies for flies.
I know the great hawk, all the feathers,
The bead names. Now, in the dryness, squaws die

Bent over their children.
I see time winding down the prairie,
White tornado, white feather straight on its spine.

I sit fixed in the vision
Of dry feathers we are becoming
How the cone will pick us and lift us

Leaving legend like deer tracks, and how they will track us
When we are lifted, row after row,
The splendid eagle headdress of God.

BEGGAR MAN

Our bank accounts
The pockets of other people's guilt.
Fat whales
We harpoon with our dryness.

There is no oil about us.
See this hand?
Dry cracked skin.

And our lips
When we smile our thanks,
Thanks, thanks,

Splitting,
Oozing with blood.
So we pay.

And as we walk away
The backs of our heels cracked
Black cracks
The earth filling our skin

With its greedy hands
Taking its payment down in advance.
Squeeze us; we crackle like paper.
The rich layer of fat

Under the skin, the pure gold
Drawn off,
Bathing other people's bones.
Tonight, the bones swim in it, fish.

A few coins, even in summer,
Snow-cold.
There is the warm coat of summer.

It makes people throw things off,
Buttons, money.
Winter is a tight coat.
Hands ride in their own fat,

Their own skin,
Then in the leather from creatures
Who lived fatter than us.
Too hard to grasp the coins then,

Too much trouble to fumble
With the tumblers, the buttons,
Their coats
More impregnable than safes.

So the weather steals from us
Or gives,
While we float out upon it,

Bad whalers
Sunk by each black coat
Lash of a tail,

Each white face
That turns from us,
All white whales

Spines heating like wicks
Aglow in their grease.

THIEF

The beautiful savage jaws of locks.
Lions. A lioness' eye
That has lost her cubs

And now she takes everything in
In her pride, ferocious.
I hunt. I hunt at night

And my eyes glow in the dark.
The carpet is grass.
I tread among the short trees,

The chairs. There is the cave,
Black and dark. How it waits
Behind an oil-painted face!

I can smell the bills,
Their bad breath
Where they breathe weakly

In thin air, sick cats.
I can hear the jewels
Where they breathe and rustle

Like the hills they once were.
I arch my back;
I move forward, shoeless.

I extend my claws, and my fur
Rises in a ridge on my back.
The night is a panther

Who has taken me in.
Even in their beds
These white things think.

I shall not
Let their alarms wake them.
I attach their wires

Back to the sky.
The morning will bring them
Thunder, lightning,

The black door thrown back,
The invisible beast loose in the house,
Stroking their throats.

In full light, I sleep,
Closer and opener of the seventh seal,
Sated with blood.

LAWYER

What are the ties that bind?
Paper, only paper.
Can you doubt it?
Here is this child.

He was born wrapped with his neck
In a cord. Now he is thirty;
The cord tightens again.
It is the will of his mother.

Her will lived in her body,
Mad canary in a cage,
Dead at the bars.
Now it lives in my drawer.

It has hands, long hands.
It is alive. Its heart beats
With the blood of spite
Which is stronger than life.

He is humbled; he is abased.
He rages like a coon in a trap
And his guilt is a leg
He must chew off to live.

At night he strokes his pillow
Like the head of his mother
And lies down on her skull.

And these loves, these marriages,
These children! They are stuck together
With paste, flour and water.
See me take this man

And give him to this woman,
Complete, complete.
She shall have his purse, his house,
His children, his great empty bed.

I decree that bad quicksand.
Should she take another,
This vision of money
Will vanish in steam cloud,

The radiators exploding in rooms.
When the steam clears, they are bare.
Around *this* man's neck is hung a knife,
And the tiny blonde body, a nude.

Expensive marble, bloodstains vein her skin.
Already, his eyes see through bars
Thick, black, immovable.
Should I do it?

I hand him back his heart.
A watch in a flat black box.
It runs, it ticks.
I am one of Their emissaries.

While I live,
It is my will.
I will it,
How the black gavel falls.

SOLDIER

Glory, and the opportunity for earth.
The opportunity to pull

The earth up over the chin,
To present oneself, suitor,

Covered with flowers,
To the red girl of the sun,

The black silks of the moon.
To earn an armor of crosses and coins.

To be an apartment of doors
To the armies of worms.

To be no more
Than a picket in a fence.

It is buried deep.
When the bugle sounds, it rises.

Or to be no more than a stitch
Decorating a hem.

Here, this land ends.
Here, no one must cross.

To transcend.
To move without mind,

Without legs.
So the new race begins.

Foreigner, colonizing the soil,
Flesh, conquering, atom by atom,

The earth. Alien transplant
The ground never rejects,

While the others carry their tears
In a small cup, seeking me out.

They dry, leaving the faint mark
Of salt. Their feet rest on my chest.

I hear them walk off.
I am a stone from a crumbling wall,

Familiar with moss,
Asleep on my back,

A woman, heavy with child,
And the sun screams down the sky

Over my blanket of green,
While the stars move aside

As the others swirl round my roots,
Green leaves, with a thunderous fall.

TINKER

If there is anything to fix,
I will fix it,
Though if the truth will be told
I am not known for my skill.

If you have a pot with one hole,
Mended, the pot may have two.
And there is a whole village
Where, at noon, the pendulum clocks

Chime once more than their twelve.
But this gives them more time,
Or mocks time as he goes.
And there is one I have touched

Whose great hands run back.
The people who live there
Are friends of the sun
And his dark servants, the shades.

They stand under the great clock,
Looking up.
Their faces brown and leather.
In times of eclipse,

There is no time.
They sit in the house
Moving old images.
Light pours out of the mirrors.

They are silvered to tin.
I tinker what breaks,
And later, it breaks down again.
I am the perfect machine,

The perpetual motion machine.
I break everything down.
When pots see me, they fear,
Knowing themselves guests on the grate.

And I shall tinker my heart,
That red pot, boiling with blood,
That clock without key,
Ticking the time

And now I mend it,
Red thing, under my hand
Growing with holes
An odd tick, a leak

And I wonder about God now,
And how he does,
Now, small vessel,
I am turning to clay.

DOCTOR

The rich man offers his arm to my cuff
Like a bribe.
While I watch the dial move, he tarnishes.

While I watch the scroll of peaks and valleys
On the ticker tape of his heart,
The bills in his safe and his bank

Change face, turn confederate.
He swallows my medicines like the real money.
He presses it on me, would dress me in it,

A green paper suit. At home,
Time is breaking into his four-chambered heart.
Drugged, my soldiers are asleep on the floor.

The beggar man comes, asking for nothing
But a wide open door in the wall that is air.
He unwraps the wounds on his foot,

Bandages of newpapers, rags. The maggots
Gluttonous rich. I douse them with ether.
They have kept the wound clean.

He seems to float on the air.
He does not need the ground.
There are things filling his pockets

He cannot see. They are weighing him down
From this world into another. There,
The magic capsule of the sea-blood

Will find him, the white whale.

The lawyer contracts with me.
He argues, he does research,
Finds precedents. He must get himself off.

There is no crime; there is only his body
Which is no evidence at all.
It sits straight in its chair,

Its eyes bright and clear.
I replace the needle; it sounds on the tray
Like a gavel. He leaves the office,

A man in a striped suit numbering his chest.
At the corner, he shakes himself like a dog.
He crosses the street.

He is pulling my evidence apart, into thread.
Circumstantial only, circumstantial.
The jury will not be impressed.

I am the doctor, the Indian chief.
I track the veins in the dry skin
Of my leg. I listen for the crackle

In my lung, a scout in the bush.
The weather changes in my eye.
It clouds. Storms gather in my chest.

I have visions. The tribe of the dead
Who came here for life. Now, witch doctor,
I chant my own spells

As the dry wind twists through my veins,
Picking them all up, stoppers with arms and legs
To the four doors of my heart.

VIII. Reading the Signs

READING THE SIGNS

Dear Lord, what's going on?
And you, what are you doing here?
We thought you were gone,
Taking back your ten fingers,
Ten bad promises, fed up fast,
The seventh day,
Pulling the blanket up to your cheek,
Turning your face to the wall.
Eternity. That greenish screen.

They *said* you were gone,
A travelling circus
Opening in another town,
But we thought you'd come back,
So there was no reason to complain.

Of course, waiting, we watched all the wrong things,
How smoke hung in the air like a brain,
Convoluted and grey,
Then dissolved into corners to think,
Or how the butterflies flew up to the sun
In a halo of ink.
We thought we were dreaming our dreams.

Wrong! the earth is not ours yet,
The whole thing is smudged with your prints,
And we saw it once, then once more,
And the world was dead, like a metaphor.
Still, your miracles are coming through

Like wet underpaint,
And your children still fear to sleep,
So you tell the same stories,
Over and over, like beads.
The burning bush used to be good,
And it's still pretty new, the river in Ohio
Filled with its flammable wastes,
Lapping at the shore with its flammable tongues,

A dragon no knight can slay,
And if the bushes aren't burning,
They will be, some day.
We will have to flood the fire with earth,
And if the seas don't divide,
You've filled them with mechanical fish,
And daily, Jonah patrols in the entrails of the whale.
It picks him up, obedient as a bus or a train.

And as for Abraham and his son,
Everyone knows that one.
The dailies tell it again and again,
And we don't forget how, once, you had the seas
Hold hands across the green belly of earth,
Though now we fear something else from the skies.

You made us too afraid of the dark.
You should have taught us to lie down,
Quiet, like the Indian,

How to pull the green quilt up over our chins
And our heads,
How to take down under the earth
The very best of the house,
Down with our bones taking their root.
And the child could begin, new,
Like a seed in the soil,
Splashing in water that doesn't divide,
Kneeling by the bush flickering like fire
In the full of the fall,

And during the last long night,
The moon would sing to him,
And the hands of the trees would come
With their leaves
And minister to the body with compresses of earth,
And the walnuts would fall
From the trees like so many minds,
And the earth would take them in,
And be wise,
And the fevers and chills go back,
Little rivulets,
To the great basins of heat and of chill,
The snows and the sun, their stories
Published each year in the leaves.

As for us, we have your book.
Our rehearsals leave nothing to chance.
It will end in fire, you said,
And we are getting prepared.
In the cities, our eyes are beginning to burn.
Our rockets are splitting the sky, red as a sea.
We are sacrificing our sons,
And the clouds have nothing to say, or else they approve.
Everyone is doing his part.
Some of us are smoking in bed,
Or throwing fire from a hose into trees,
And the trees are twisting their roots.
Their leaves, little hands, will not keep releasing
The clean air into the sky like invisible birds.

But it's different, now that we know you are here.
You needed us in the dark, holding your hand.
It's really on the fifth day, or maybe the sixth.
Come in, stick around.
Take off your coat; wiggle your toes.
Sit in front of the hearth,
Or warm your hands at the stove,
Four blue beasts,
Flexing themselves at the turn of a switch.

More and more of the earth is turning to ash,
Is sifted through with thin splinters of glass.
We are dreaming your dreams.
We will see to it all, before we lie down.

THE NATURE OF GENRES

A big room.
One-hundred women
At one-hundred desks
Bend their heads

Over their pens.
The sky runs with ink.
At night,
The man who enters

Collects one-hundred rhymed worlds;
Their horizons are flat.

Somewhere, the sound of thunder.
The raised muzzles of guns.
Explosions occur.
There is danger.

There is a request
For one round world.
The one-hundred identical girls
Form one straight line

And melt into one.
This is the priority of war.
The one girl holds her head.
She is a shoe factory

Converted for weapons.
She is a mother
Of a baby who will not go to sleep.
She leaves it bits of paper.

It will not eat
Unless she stays with it.
Each page that she writes
Is a plate in its skull.

Each page that she writes
Extends the horizon
Which still remains flat.
The fleet sails over, is lost.

She cannot sleep.
She wakes
Hearing it breathe in the dark.
It makes no sound at all.

She feeds it, page after page.
As her own world grows flatter,
Its world starts to curve.
One day, the ships sail back

Full of banners, their crews
Green Indians
With emerald eyes.
The world is rounding,

And starting to spin.
She is one-hundred girls
Bent over a desk.
The part in her hair

Is perfectly straight,
One-hundred sleek heads.
At night,
The man takes the one-hundred

White worlds.
Their horizons are flat.

She has been God.
Her fingerprints are gone.
They are blank as a page.
She is starting again.

The round world
Turned to dry ice as it spun.
Her fingers tore loose.
Now it warms in the sky.

Her round sobbings begin.

NOVELIST

The tips of your fingers grow wise;
You are picking the safe of the air.
The policeman goes by.
Bolder now, you tap

The telephone line to the heart.
The best things are said in a sleep.
You are reading the runes in the dust.
You have it now,

Precious and faceted and red.
You have the surgeon's boiled hands.
Once planted, your wax dolls
Quicken and stand.

Meanwhile, the model goes on with its life.
Its hair stiffens and curls.
Does the automatic alarm
Expensive, expensive,

Go off at the edge of the lawn?
Do the police rush in,
Time after time?
Do they feel the draft at the heart?

Does a small shutter
Open a corridor of bright light,
Blinding, square,
Windowing the brain?

They look, nothing is gone.
They are ashamed.
At night, do they dream
Of the secret drawer,

Empty and raw?
Meanwhile, you are changing
The names, like tumblers,
Like keys for a lock.

Caught now, they stare
From a black box,
Their lives revolve and repeat,
Endless,

Jammed scene in a play,
Perform without pay,
See how they claw now
At the very same sky

The stars draw in their spikes
The sky, shuttered in clouds
Day, night,
This is the crime now;

You have returned it,
All extenuations lost.

POST MORTEM

The sky is reduced,
A narrow blue ribbon banding the lake.
Someone is wrapping things up.
The curving horizon flattens to corners.
Someone is peeling back
The green parchment of the hills.
Hinged, the cherubed ceiling tilts to blankness.
The stars blink and fade.

Two fingers lift the house,
A tiny package.
Eyes shut,
I lie quiet beneath mounded quilts.
Have they marked things fragile?—
My glass bones break.

This time I hope for
Museums, pedestals,
Columns casting shadows
Themselves too heavy to move,
Even the dust heavy
In sculptured, marble light.
The movers of this life
Were not careful enough.

TIDES

That afternoon
There was an undertow in the sea of light.
The woods had thousands and thousands of doors,
But no roads. The foliage was lacy and golden and green.
We climbed down out of light into darkness.

The squirrels took an interest in us and our gifts,
As we walked among their trees like trees,
But the earth entered a monkish phase
Turning its cheek from the sun,
Powdering itself like a nun, all white.
The skies grew black as habits.
We were two threads in the pinework tapestry
When the wings of a crow cut us off.

Our footprints lasted behind us, empty as beds.
We climbed down, like spiders on string.
The rock slabs were heavy and huge,
Patterned with lichen,
Carpets of Persian, carpets of stone.
We came to the crevices,
Cold fissures in earth flesh, the grey cathedrals,
Upside down. At night, the bats
Worshipped beside us on prayer rugs of stone.

Hunters still knock at our doors near the bowl's edge.
We would tell them, go back,
How all the cave mouths are open
To the salt sea's communion, and how,
At their back, a mendicant sleeps,
Curled up like a tongue,
His errand forgotten, though the tide rushes in.
We would tell them, go back,
How near we are to them,
How the squirrels step through us, but the wind
Keeps blowing the leaves up under our chins
Like years.

BURIAL GROUND

Elephant-skinned trees, a tumble
Of cold stones, a litter of leaves
And beyond these
The cemetery's neat grey rows.
Against a pale grey sky
A stone-cold angel lifts her granite hand,
Her full skirts
Unruffled by the wintry breeze, and at her feet
A small squirrel buries his sweet fruit.
He does not mark the place with stone
Or twig, nor do his beady eyes read
The inscription on the stone.
He knows what he knows.
The nut will be dug up.
The roots of the trees go deep.
They remember the sun and the rain.
We have no roots. We do not remember long.
We bury our dead
And carve their names in stone.

POETRY WRITING

And this is poking through ashes
In ruined country,
And this is how one does it,
And yes, the twice-burned hand returns
To the fire,
And this is what it finds there:
These charred forms, twisted
Like driftwood, lovely,
The old pain
Gone
With the gone flames, they still burn—
But flames
In a mirror; they hurt
Your mind's eyes,
And the ashes float on the air; they settle
Like black snow
On the plains and grasses,
And this is how you know my life burned
This way,
The cat's prints
A trifle blacker
On the clean and driven snow.

WEDDING RING POEM

If you wake up
And go about all day
And find your wedding ring

And engagement ring
Asleep in the sheets,
Is it a sign?

If you brush your hair
And small swallows fly out,
Is it a sign?

If you sleep on your back
And find a tiny glass deer
In your belly button,

Curled up;
If your bones turn to gold;
If your lashes

Cover radioactive eyes;
If a nail breaks and splits,
And a tiny thorn

Grows in its place;
If you learn to fly in the dark;
If you wake up

With a green tongue
Speaking Abyssinian and Greek;
If a hummingbird follows you home;

If the moon gets stuck in your tree;
If over your home
There are only red suns,

Is it a sign?
Is it enough?
Is it ever enough?